TEENS IN CANADA

Teens in

CANADA

by Kitty Shea

Content Adviser: Miriam Kaufman, M.D.,
Associate Professor, University of Toronto

Reading Adviser: Katie Van Sluys, Ph.D.,
Department of Teacher Education,
DePaul University

Compass Point Books ✦ Minneapolis, Minnesota

Compass Point Books
151 Good Counsel Drive
P.O. Box 669
Mankato, MN 56002-0669

Editor: Mari Bolte
Designers: The Design Lab and Jaime Martens
Photo Researcher: Eric Gohl
Cartographer: XNR Productions, Inc.
Library Consultant: Kathleen Baxter

Art Director: Jaime Martens
Creative Director: Keith Griffin
Editorial Director: Nick Healy
Managing Editor: Catherine Neitge

Library of Congress Cataloging-in-Publication Data
Shea, Kitty.
 Teens in Canada / by Kitty Shea.
   p. cm. — (Global connections)
 Includes bibliographical references and index.
 ISBN: 978-0-7565-3303-8 (library binding)
 ISBN: 978-0-7565-3304-5 (paperback)
   1. Teenagers—Canada—Social conditions—21st century—Juvenile literature.
   2. Teenagers—Canada—Social life and customs—21st century—Juvenile literature.
   I. Title. II. Series.
 HQ799.C2S44 2008
  305.2350971—dc22   2007004899

Visit Compass Point Books on the Internet at www.compasspointbooks.com
or e-mail your request to custserv@compasspointbooks.com

Table of Contents

PACIFIC

CANADA

UNITED STATES OF AMER

MEXICO

Ottawa

OCEAN

ATLANTIC

OCEAN

GREENLAND

ICELAND

DENMARK
GERMANY
NETH.
BELGIUM
U.K.
IRELAND
FRANCE
ITALY
PORTUGAL
SPAIN
MOROCCO
TUNISIA

SENEGAL
GUINEA

THE BAHAMAS

CUBA
HAITI
DOM. REP.
JAMAICA

ONDURAS
ICARAGUA
STA RICA
PANAMA

COLOMBIA

BRAZIL

ECUADOR

L00 New Potato

ALARM CLOCKS BUZZ. CLOCK RADIOS BLARE. Parents call, "Time to wake up!" Some announce the day's beginning in French: "Bonjour! Jus d'orange?" or "Good morning! Orange juice?" Canada is second only to Russia in physical size but ranks 28th in population. Wake-up calls roll like falling dominos across Canada's 3,200 miles (5,120 kilometers). So begins a new day in Canada.

It takes four and a half hours to rouse all 2.5 million of Canada's 9- to 14-year-olds—not because they're lazy or especially tired, but because the country, with its 10 provinces and three territories, is so large it spans six time zones. This means that 7 A.M. in Canada's easternmost territory, Newfoundland, is only 2:30 A.M. in the far-west province of British Columbia. By the time British Columbians begin waking up, the Newfoundlanders have finished lunch and are back to work.

"Get up now!" parents prod. The maple syrup is on the table—Canada produces about 85 percent of the world's supply—and the pancakes are on the plate. Early-morning hockey practice means it's out of bed and out the door for the teens who play Canada's national game. Everyone else gets to sleep a little longer.

There are more than 15,500 elementary and secondary schools throughout Canada.

CHAPTER ONE

Meters & "Merci"

YAWNS ARE CATCHY AT THE BUS STOP. A bundled-up teen girl wearing a toque, Canada's national winter hat, lets out a big yawn as she shifts from one booted foot to the other, trying to get warm. The hot tea she drank at breakfast isn't helping a wink against this wind chill. Like half of Canadians ages 9 to 14, she drinks tea because it's trendy and fun. More than 75 percent of all Canadians drink some sort of tea. Why, she wonders, can't her family move to Canada's west coast, where the winters are balmy? The average temperature in more than two-thirds of Canada is minus 1 degree Fahrenheit (minus 18 degrees Celsius) in January.

Several paces away, a boy leans against his snowboard and stifles his own yawn. His stomach is growling. He'd poured himself a bowl of Shreddies, a Chex-like cereal, but left it on the kitchen counter and flew out the door, thinking he was late. He wasn't.

Neighbor kids are still scurrying toward the corner as their yellow school bus appears over the rise, flashes its warning lights, and drops its red stop arm.

toque
twok-ck

"Brrrrr" at its Coldest

In February 1947, the mercury dropped out of the thermometer in Snag, Yukon, setting a North American mark for the coldest temperature on record. How cold was it? Try minus 81.4 F (minus 63 C). One of the official weather observers that day noted:

"We threw a dish of water high into the air, just to see what would happen. Before it hit the ground, it made a hissing noise, froze, and fell as tiny round pellets of ice the size of wheat kernels."

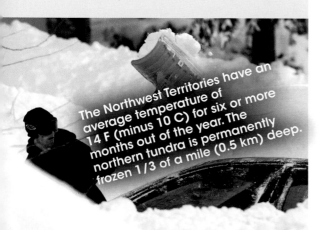

The Northwest Territories have an average temperature of 14 F (minus 10 C) for six or more months out of the year. The northern tundra is permanently frozen 1/3 of a mile (0.5 km) deep.

Every day, 36,800 buses provide transportation to Canada's K-12 students.

Waking up and yawning, hurrying up and waiting: Such is the scene that unfolds for Canadian teens every Monday through Friday morning during the school year, which runs from September until June.

Not Just One School System

Canada is divided into 10 provinces and three territories, and school systems differ from one to the next. Provinces function independently but within the framework of Canadian law, calling their own shots on education, health care, transportation, and welfare. The federal government handles these matters in the Yukon and Northwest Territories. The Inuit people, whose ancestors were among Canada's first settlers 5,000 years ago, govern the territory of Nunavut.

As with public school students nationwide, the bus stop crowd attends school at no cost. Education is likewise free at government-supported parochial schools—called separate schools—that are run by Roman Catholic and Protestant organizations. These schools include religion classes in their curricula. Not all provinces have parochial schools.

Private schools, on the other hand, come with a tuition bill. They're the schools of choice for about 5 percent of Canadian students and their families. About 2 percent of Canadian students receive their education at home.

Provinces East to West

Newfoundland and Labrador
Atlantic provinces are iceberg country in the spring. Newfoundland, "The Rock," is an island, and Labrador is the mainland. Both provinces are home to four aboriginal groups and both have namesake dogs.

Nova Scotia
Scottish heritage infuses this Atlantic province, which is connected to mainland North America by only a sliver of land. *Titanic* survivors were brought to its capital of Halifax in 1912.

Prince Edward Island
This Atlantic province is Canada's smallest in land and population. Accessed via a nine-mile (14.4 km) bridge, by ferry, or by airplane.

New Brunswick
Densely forested Atlantic, or Maritime, province is surrounded by water on three sides and Maine on its fourth. Lobster is fishing industry's main catch.

Quebec
Canada's largest province was settled by the French 300 years ago and continues to be defined by French culture and French-speaking residents.

Ontario
Canada's wealthiest and most populated province includes nation's capital Ottawa, business hub Toronto, and tourist magnet Niagara Falls.

Manitoba
Prairie province is called "the land of 100,000 lakes." Its city Churchill is visited annually by polar bears en route to ice fields farther north.

Saskatchewan
Flat prairie province is a huge wheat producer. Archaeological digs have turned up fossils, including a nearly complete Tyrannosaurus rex skeleton.

Alberta
Mountain ranges give it spectacular scenery around Banff, Jasper, and Lake Louise. Oil and natural gas drilling provide its wealth.

British Columbia
The "Gateway to the Pacific," its city Vancouver has a significant Asian population. It's also the location of the 2010 Winter Olympic Games.

Territories East to West

Nunavut
Established in 1999 and governed by the Inuit, it covers one-fifth of Canada. No roads exist between Nunavut and the rest of Canada.

Northwest Territories
Only about 41,000 people, half of whom are aboriginal, live across its 468,000 square miles (1.17 million sq. km). During the summer, the sun shines 24 hours.

Yukon
Famous for the Klondike gold rush, its landscape is mostly mountains and tundra. Only four of its communities have more than 500 residents, and approximately one in five Yukon residents are under the age of 15.

With only 25 percent of aboriginal students finishing high school, improving their educational outcomes is one of Canada's goals.

Canadian children first hop on the bus and begin their grade-one education at age 6, although some may already have preschool, junior kindergarten, or kindergarten under their belts. Early childhood offerings differ by province or territory. Canadian students remain in elementary school until grade five to grade eight, depending on where they live. Some provinces group grades six through eight in senior elementary schools, which are like middle schools, bridging elementary school and high school. Other provinces cluster grades seven, eight, and often nine in junior high schools. In most provinces, Canadian students are required to attend *école secondaire,* or high school, until they are 16 or 18.

Kids big and little can seem half-asleep on the bus ride to school. The award for being the groggiest, however, goes to the students who live the farthest

école secondaire
a-KOHL SAY-kon-dare

away and must get picked up extremely early. Other students whose families live in faraway parts of Canada may attend boarding schools, staying overnight at school during the week and going home on weekends and holidays. Students in outlying areas can also "go" to school without actually going anywhere by

Teen Scenes

It's late morning on Prince Edward Island. A 14-year-old boy wakes up at 8 A.M., long after his neighbors have wolfed down breakfast and run to catch the bus. He doesn't bother to get dressed as he walks downstairs to fix himself a bowl of cereal and a glass of juice. He can wake up at a leisurely pace because he has nowhere to rush to: His parents homeschool him. But that doesn't mean that he has less work than other students. When your mom's the teacher, not doing your homework could mean more than detention!

On a reserve in Nunavut, a 15-year-old First Nations girl wakes up while the sky is still dark. She helps her mother prepare a breakfast of fish and bannock, a type of fried bread. She helps wake the rest of the house before catching a bus to her school, 45 minutes away from the reserve. It's far, but it's a good school. The girl hopes to attend an aboriginal college and then get a job improving the lives of the First Nations people. After school, she usually meets with a relative who lives on the reserve who teaches her his native aboriginal language.

Provinces away, a 15-year-old girl hurries to join her friends at school in Alberta for an early breakfast of a ham and cheese English muffin. The breakfast is provided by the Quebec Breakfast Club, a nutrition program that serves more than 2 million breakfasts to students a year. Later the girl and her friends will head off to class to study French, Spanish, and English. Her parents have promised that she can study abroad in Europe after high school if she gets good grades.

These Canadian teens lead different lives and look forward to different futures. But it's this diversity that makes Canada a country of many unified cultures.

doing their coursework and studying online.

Learning Languages

Canadian students likely learn a second language at school, with English-speaking students, or Anglophones, taking French class while Francophones, or French-speaking students, study English. Canada is one of the few countries in the world that is officially bilingual. Thus, signs at its borders read "Welcome to Canada/Bienvenue au Canada," certain boxes of cereal are labeled Captain Crunch/Capitaine Crounche, and official Web sites have visitors specify English or Français. Exiting the bus, students call "Thank you" or "*Merci*" to their driver. Tripping over their friend's foot in the hallway, it's "Sorry" or "*Désolé*." Upon entering the classroom, they greet teachers with "Hi" or "*Bonjour*."

For the aboriginal groups in Canada, running their own schools allows them to preserve their native language and culture. Because Inuit children were forced by the government during the first half of the 20th century to speak the national languages of English or French, the Inuits' native language of Inuktitut was being used less, putting it at risk of being forgotten entirely. Today Inuit educators strive to salvage the language by promoting Inuktitut study in schools and encouraging parents to speak it at home.

Even the English that's taught in Canada comes with a built-in history lesson. Canadian English has its origins

Check Your Spelling

English-speaking Canadians use the British spellings of certain words when reading and writing, which is helpful to know before taking a spelling test in Canada.

U.S.	Canada
Behavior	Behaviour
Catalog	Catalogue
Color	Colour
Check	Cheque
Center	Centre
Favorite	Favourite
Honor	Honour
Labor	Labour
Neighbor	Neighbour
Theater	Theatre

merci
mare-see

désolé
day-so-lay

bonjour
bohn-joor

ROYAL VICTORIA   ROYAL VICTORIA

Hôpital · Hospital   Hôpital · Hospital

← Entrées de l'hôpital   ↑ Entrées de l'hôpital

Hospital Entrances   Hospital Entrances

Stationnement ℗ Parking   Stationnement ℗ Parking

↑ URGENCE   → URGENCE

EMERGENCY   EMERGENCY

↑ Livraison · Receiving   → Livraison · Receiving

Many signs in Canada, primarily in Quebec and Montreal, are written in both French and English.

in Great Britain and doesn't stray very far from the British version of English, grammatically speaking. But Canadian students who read materials published in the United States might notice that some words are spelled differently. Canada, like the other former British territories Australia and New Zealand, officially uses the British English language spelling traditions.

All in a (School) Day's Work

Many Canadian students start their school day by listening to Canada's national anthem over the public address system or singing it themselves. As the day unfolds, they turn their attention to math, science, social studies, language arts, the fine arts, and physical education. Each province or territory has its own official curriculum, or program of studies, that students in each grade must know before being promoted to the next grade. The curriculum specifies the textbooks being used and which end-of-year exams must be taken.

Grade-five math students in Ontario, for instance, are expected to master adding and subtracting decimal amounts to hundredths, converting meters to centimeters and kilometers to meters, and measuring angles to 90 degrees with a protractor. They also study patterning, algebra, and data management.

In Alberta, grade-six students in science class tackle airflow and aerodynamics, flight, sky science, evidence

"O Canada!"

Sung or listened to daily in classrooms across Canada, the country's national anthem is also performed before public events and when Canada's Olympians (often the hockey teams) win the gold.

O Canada!

Our home and native land!
True patriot love in all thy sons command.

With glowing hearts we see thee rise.
The True North strong and free!

From far and wide,
O Canada, we stand on guard for thee.

God keep our land glorious and free!
O Canada, we stand on guard for thee.

O Canada, we stand on guard for thee.

Measuring With Metrics

Like every country in the world except the United States, Burma, and Liberia, Canada uses the metric system. To keep things interesting, Canadians make an exception and quote their height in feet/inches and weight in pounds.

Wondering how much farther? 1 kilometer = 0.62 mile	
Learning how to drive? 100 km per hour = 62 miles per hour	
Dying of thirst? 1 liter soda = 33.8 ounces	
Buying trail mix in bulk? 1 kilogram = 2.2 pounds	
Wishing you'd worn another layer? 0 degrees Celsius = 32 degrees Fahrenheit	

and investigation, and trees and forests. Seventh-grade social studies students may study Canadian and world history, geography, and current events.

The basics behind them, high school students choose to concentrate on studies that prepare them to pursue a degree at a university, a hands-on trade at a college or technical school, or a job in the workplace. More than 70 percent of parents expect their children to attend a university. Most

There is a high dropout rate in students participating in physical education courses once they reach grade 10, when the subject is no longer mandatory.

In 2004, 97.7 percent of all elementary and secondary schools had access to computers.

Canadian high schools use the semester system: Fall/winter term runs from September through January, with spring term continuing from February until June. The school day for many high-schoolers is broken down into four to six class periods plus one for lunch.

Speaking of lunch, Canadian students either dig into bag lunches from home or buy lunch at school. Cafeteria menus include fast-food favorites such as submarine sandwiches, pepperoni pizza, and chicken nuggets. They may also feature dishes such as

a crush of students spills out. About one-quarter of them hustle off to soccer practice, swimming lessons, or other after-school activities. Their classmates who ride the bus climb aboard, jostle for seats, and settle in for the trip home.

Dropout Rates

Although high school graduation rates continue to increase in Canada, there are still those who choose not to, or are unable to, finish high school. Students who don't graduate are left with few options. A high school diploma is the minimum level of education required for many jobs, and workers who don't have diplomas make less money, work in less ideal jobs, and have poorer health than workers who finished high school. In 2004-2005, only 62 percent of dropouts were employed. However, some of these students choose to continue their education at a later time. In 2002, 11 percent of dropouts had returned to high school and another 16 percent had continued their education at secondary school.

soups, pastas, and meatballs. In smaller communities, students who live within walking distance of their schools might go home for lunch—with permission, of course.

When the dismissal bell rings at day's end, school doors fling open and

There are more than 700,000 registered snowmobiles and nearly 100,000 miles (161,000 km) of snowmobiling trails throughout the country. Snowmobiles serve as both recreational vehicles and means of transportation.

2

Civilized in its Own Way

THE BUS RIDE HOME IS LOUDER AND LIVELIER THAN THE MORNING TRIP TO SCHOOL. Passengers sing out loud or play air drums with pencils as they groove to the bands Our Lady Peace, Barenaked Ladies, and The Tragically Hip through mp3 players. They dig through their knapsacks for Smarties, which are like extra-sweet M&Ms, or for Coffee Crisp, Mr. Big, Aero, and Caramilk chocolate bars. One boy bets his seatmate that the Montreal Canadiens will clobber the Toronto Maple Leafs in the upcoming National Hockey League game. His pal, a fanatic Leafs fan, takes him up on the

challenge. Two girls slump in their seat and giggle over the latest Vervegirl, a favorite Canadian teen magazine.

The bus driver navigates the city streets cautiously. There's considerable traffic despite public transit systems that include such alternatives as buses, subways, light-rail lines, trolleys, ferries, and trains. Nearly 80 percent of Canadians own one vehicle, while 36 percent own two or more, sometimes designating the second one for winter use and dubbing it the "beater with a heater." Vehicles in Canada have electrical plugs sticking out from under their hoods. These are attached to special

23

heaters that keep the engines in parked vehicles warm enough for early start ing. In areas with the harshest winters, snowmobiles are a common means of transportation.

The school bus pulls over and riders file out. City kids shuffle down sidewalks past corner stores and toward stand-alone houses, row houses, or high-rise apartments. Eighty percent of Canadians live in urban areas, with the balance residing in the country. More than half of all Canadians have pets, so there's a lot of commotion when students make their way up the front steps and announce "I'm home!"

Welcome Home

Home-ownership is a reality for 62 percent of Canadians. Almost all Canadian homes are outfitted with color TVs, telephones, compact-disc players, dishwashers, and microwaves that run on electricity. Canadian homes look like most residences in Westernized countries, although the rooms, furnishings, and appliances might have different names. Bathrooms are "washrooms," and the garbage disposal is known as the "garburator."

Canadians call their southern neighbors "the States," reasoning that Canadians are just as American as Americans are. The United States has

Humans and animals often have close encounters in Canada's rural and wilderness areas.

The St. Lawrence River allows access to 15 U.S. and Canadian ports.

considerable influence globally because of its economic, political, and military might. Its impact on Canada's economy and culture is especially keen because the countries are so close and the U.S. population is much greater than Canada's. Canada's southern border is shared with the United States, creating the longest shared border in the world at 3,138 miles (5,061 m) long. About 90 percent of Canada's population lives within 100 miles (161 km) of the border. Residents of Canada's capital city, Ottawa, can zip to the United States in an hour and a half by car. There's a U.S. border to Canada's northwest as well: Alaska.

Canada may be in North America, but it's a mistake to think of it as "North" America. Canada is very much its own country. It is larger geographically and far less populated. The United States has nine times as many residents, with 82.2 per square mile (32.9 people per square kilometer); whereas Canada has an average of 9.2 people per square mile (3.7 per square kilometer), which is one of the lowest population densities in the world. Canada thus earns its reputation

The Peace Arch Park lies in Blaine, Washington, and Douglas, British Columbia. The park allows visitors to spend time on both U.S. and Canadian soil and brings year-round tourists to the surrounding areas.

for being a last frontier. Only about 5 percent of the land is suitable for agriculture. This means that in most of the country, there are no shopping malls, no fast-food restaurants, no anything that gets in the way of 1,300-pound (585 kilogram) polar bears padding across the Arctic tundra, cranky grizzly bears nosing around the forests, 1,000-pound (450 kg) moose lumbering across the prairies, and agile cougars patrolling the Canadian Rockies, Coast Mountains, and other ranges.

Canada stands out for its progressive policies concerning health care and education, too. The government pays for health care, ensuring that everyone receives the same quality of care.

However, some residents complain about the quality of the health care, questioning the efficiency of the system to deliver medications and treatments in a timely fashion. Those in rural areas have limited medical access, and other patients have reported that the average wait for an elective, or planned, nonemergency, surgery in Canada is 18 weeks—and would be even longer if desperate patients didn't have access to medical treatments in the United States. Canadian Chief Justice Beverly McLachlin points out that "access to a waiting list is not access to health care."

Regardless of how they feel,

Canada
Population density
and political map

Population Density
(People per square km)

More than 100
50–100
10–49
1–9
Less than 1

ARCTIC OCEAN

GREENLAND
(Denmark)

Beaufort
Sea

Baffin
Bay

Labrador
Sea

UNITED STATES

YUKON
• Whitehorse

NORTHWEST
TERRITORIES
• Yellowknife

NUNAVUT

Iqaluit •

NEWFOUNDLAND AND
LABRADOR

St. John's •

Hudson
Bay

BRITISH
COLUMBIA

ALBERTA

SASKATCHEWAN

MANITOBA

QUEBEC

PRINCE EDWARD
ISLAND
• Charlottetown
NOVA SCOTIA

PACIFIC
OCEAN

• Edmonton

ONTARIO

Fredericton •
Quebec •

Halifax •

Vancouver •
• Calgary

Victoria •

• Regina
• Winnipeg

Montreal •
Ottawa •

NEW BRUNSWICK

UNITED STATES

ATLANTIC
OCEAN

Toronto •

0   200   400 mi.
0   200   400 km

N
W   E
S

Canadians have one of the highest life expectancies in the world, with an average of about 80 years.

KitchenTable Business

Canadian teens are reminded almost nightly that theirs is a country that values education: The country's 99 percent literacy rate proves it. Education in grades K-12 is free to all Canadian citizens and permanent residents.

Two out of three students usually have homework. Canadian teens have been known to use academic performance as a bargaining tool to get what they want from their parents—say, track pants and a fleece hoodie from Roots, a Canadian retailer whose fashions celebrate Canada.

Money in Your Pocket

Canadian coins are like a trip to the zoo. Nickels feature a beaver. Quarters have a caribou. The star of the $1 gold-colored loonie coin is, yes, a common loon. The $2 twoonie (sometimes spelled "toonie") boasts a polar bear against gold set inside a silver frame. Pennies and dimes feature a maple leaf and the *Bluenose*, a famous schooner, respectively. One-dollar bills are no longer being printed but are still accepted by retailers.

Canadian money comes in variety of colors: $5 is blue, $10 is purple, $20 is green, $50 is red, and $100 is brown.

As well as serving donuts, the popular Tim Hortons chain offers muffins, soup, cookies, and sandwiches.

Doing Donuts

Canada has more donut stores per capita than anywhere else on the planet. Not coincidentally, its citizens devour the most donuts, too. Tim Hortons feeds the demand with its 2,700-plus donut shops in Canada. The sugar-frosted chain is so popular that its trademark phrase—"Double double," or a coffee with two creams and two sugars—was recently added to the *Canadian Oxford Dictionary*.

"It's an unpretentious brand," said Cathy Whelan Malloy, director of advertising for Tim Hortons. "It's very similar to how you would think of a Canadian: friendly, caring, dependable. That's our brand character."

The late Tim Horton was a household name in Canada even before Canadians got a taste of his namesake treats. He played on four Stanley Cup-winning Toronto Maple Leafs teams during his 22-year professional hockey career.

Three out of four Canadian parents give in if their teens' pleas are linked to improved grades or other achievements. Another teen tactic is to chip in part of a desired item's cost by drawing from their allowance, which, for about half of 9- to 14-year-olds, amounts to $9.20 in Canadian dollars (U.S.$8.60) weekly. Even more young teens have bank accounts of their own.

Homework done, teens and their families tackle the night's big question: "What's for dinner?" After school, teens commonly chow down on donuts, butter tarts (similar to pecan pie, without the pecans), or ketchup chips. Provided they still have an appetite, dinner might be a dish that's unique to Canada and, often, to the particular region in which they live. Canada has a diverse selection of food choices: Montreal alone has more than 5,000 restaurants that serve 75 types of cuisine.

Seafood dishes are naturals in the Atlantic provinces and in British Columbia on the Pacific side. French-Canadians prepare *soupe aux pois*, or yellow pea soup, or they might grab a *tourtiére* at the grocery store,

even though the spiced meat pie is usually served on Christmas Eve and New Year's Eve. Residents of New Brunswick gather fiddleheads in the forest come springtime, boiling the coiled fern shoots and serving them with lemon and butter. In the Arctic, meals are often built around such wild game as caribou, moose, and bear. Macaroni and cheese is a hit from sea to sea. Canadians call it "Kraft Dinner" regardless of the boxed brand used. They proudly consume more "KD" than any nationality on Earth. More than 7 million of these blue-and-orange boxes are sold each week worldwide, 1.7 million of those coming from sales in Canada alone.

When a teen is hungry as a bear, going out to eat is a good option. Burgers from Harvey's, submarine

soupe aux pois
soop o PWA

tourtiére
tor-tee-AIR

Lobster is Canada's most valuable seafood export, contributing $1 billion (U.S.$934 million) to the industry a year. Consumers from 55 countries feast on lobster caught in Canadian waters.

Although there are many variations of poutine, including recipes with shredded cheese, mashed potatoes, and meat, the original poutine is a classic comfort food.

poutine
pout-san

sandwiches from Mr. Sub, and pizza from Boston Pizza are on Canada's fast-food menu. Smorgasbords serving Canadian Chinese cuisine, or Can/Chinese, dot the landscape, as do eateries selling *poutine*—cheese curds plopped atop french fries and drowned in gravy—a dish that originated in Quebec but can now be found at places as common as McDonald's or Burger King. Canadians get a table at The Keg for steak dinners or at Swiss Chalet for chicken and ribs. Ordering a side of chips, otherwise known as french fries? They come with malt vinegar or gravy and ketchup. Ordering a beer? You must be 18 years old in Quebec, Manitoba, or Alberta, and 19 elsewhere. Pop is what you get if you leave your ID at home.

Can-ada

A soft drink is called "pop" in Canada, although some Canadians refer to it as "coke" or "soft drink." In 2007, a loonie would buy you a can of pop from a vending machine in most parts of Canada, except for university campuses and popular tourist areas. Mountain Dew is made in Canada without caffeine, because health regulations allow caffeine in dark, colalike drinks only. A caffeinated version, called Dew Fuel, is allowed because it is marketed as a natural health product and not as a soft drink. The legendary ginger ale Canada Dry traces its roots to the southern Ontario city of Toronto.

31

The number of single-parent households has slowly been increasing over the last 20 years.

3

Room Enough for Everyone

WEEKENDS ARF ONE OF THE FEW TIMES DURING THE SCHOOL YEAR WHEN TEENS CAN SLEEP LATE, an opportunity much appreciated by a gang of friends who stayed up late watching movies. (Hayden Christensen, the actor who plays Anakin Skywalker/Darth Vader in Episodes II and III of the Star Wars series, is just one of many Canadians who have made it big.) Granted, sleeping in on Saturday mornings means zoning out the racket of mothers doing laundry and vacuuming—Canadian women generally do more of the housework than men—but at least there aren't alarm clocks beeping, school buses to catch, or classes to attend.

Canadian families are on the small side, with an average family in Canada having three people: two parents and one child. Fewer bodies to mess up a house are a bonus for those who do the housework. More than half of Canadian teens today are expected to pitch in with household chores.

Canadian Exports

Canada has given the world artistic talent enough to crowd a red carpet. Ontario is Canada's most populated province, which might explain its high output of celebrities relative to the other provinces.

Singer/Songwriter	Birthplace	Famous For
Bryan Adams	Kingston, Ontario	"Everything I Do (I Do It For You)"
Celine Dion	Charlemagne, Quebec	"My Heart Will Go On"
Nelly Furtado	Victoria, British Columbia	"I'm Like a Bird"
k.d. lang	Edmonton, Alberta	"Constant Craving"
Diana Krall	Nanaimo, British Columbia	"Temptation"
Avril Lavigne	Napanee, Ontario	"Sk8er Boi"
Sarah McLachlan	Halifax, Nova Scotia	"Angel"
Alanis Morissette	Ottawa, Ontario	"Ironic"
Shania Twain	Windsor, Ontario	"Man! I Feel Like a Woman"
Neil Young	Toronto, Ontario	"Rockin' in the Free World"

Actor/Comedian	Birthplace	Famous For
Hayden Christensen	Vancouver, British Columbia	*Star Wars, Episodes II and III*
Dan Aykroyd	Ottawa, Ontario	*Blues Brothers*
Jim Carrey	Newmarket, Ontario	*Dumb and Dumber*
Michael J. Fox	Edmonton, Alberta	*Back to The Future*
Eugene Levy	Hamilton, Ontario	*American Pie*
Mike Myers	Scarborough, Ontario	*Austin Powers*
William Shatner	Montreal, Quebec	*Star Trek*

Typical and Not

Living under one roof with mom and dad is common: Three out of four Canadian children live in homes headed by two parents, which isn't to say their parents all have marriage certificates. Throughout Canada, 14 percent of unions are common-law marriages; in Quebec, it's more than 30 percent. Common-law couples live together and, in most provinces, share legal rights, but they don't have a marriage license.

Families take many shapes in Canada. It's common for a class at school to include students from single-parent homes as well as homes in which two families combined after parents remarried. Two percent of Canadian households are either multigenerational—grandparents, parents, and children under one roof—or skip-generation households in which grandparents fill in for absent parents. One nice thing about these arrangements is that, as the generation gap narrows, it's easier to get to know grandma and grandpa.

Not that confrontations with parents aren't possible. From ages 10

Although the family makeup of Canada is changing, two-parent families remain the most common.

Same-sex Marriages

"We will send a statement to the world that in Canada gays and lesbians will not be considered second-class citizens," Michael Savage, a member of Parliament, said in 2006. From 2003 to 2006, more than 12,000 same-sex couples were married in Canada. Canada became the third country in the world (after Belgium and the Netherlands) to give nationwide recognition to same-sex couples.

Second-parent adoption, or the legal adoption of a child by a same-sex partner, has been allowed in Canada since 1994. This means that some teens may have two moms or two dads ruling their household.

Many couples from the United States, where same-sex marriage is not yet accepted, travel to Canada to be married. Couples don't need to be Canadian citizens to be granted a marriage license in Canada.

Canada has elected several gay politicians to office, including Libby Davies, the first gay female member of Parliament, Svend Robinson, former member of Parliament and gay rights activist, and Scott Brison, the first openly gay Cabinet member.

Top 10 Baby Names in Canada (2004-2005)

Girls	Boys
Emma	Ethan/Ethen
Emily/Emilie	Matthew
Sarah/Sara	Joshua
Madison/Madisyn	Jacob/Jakob
Hannah/Hanna	Nicholas/Nickolas
Olivia	Aidan/Aiden
Hailey/Hayley	Ryan
Maya/Mia	Alexander
Kaitlyn/Katelyn	Nathan
Abigail/Abigayle	Benjamin

until 15, young Canadians say their relationships with their parents slide. Problems bubble up when, for instance, teens slack on their schoolwork or don't wear seat belts or bike helmets. Smoking cigarettes, drinking alcohol, or hanging out with kids who use drugs are big-deal issues as well. Canadian moms are more likely to hear about their children's troubles: Sons and daughters confide in their mothers to the same degree. Boys, however, are more likely to talk to their fathers than are girls. A recent study found that Canadian teens look up to their parents as a source of information, and, as much as they may deny it, are willing to follow their parents' advice.

A Country of Differences

More than 200 ethnicities are represented in Canada's population. About 14 percent are members of a visible minority group—meaning not Caucasian and not from an aboriginal group, but possibly, but not necessarily, from mixed backgrounds—and immigration accounts for more than 50 percent of Canada's population growth. Many immigrants come from Asia and the Middle East. It has been projected that after the year 2025, Canada's population growth will be based entirely on immigration.

Canada even devotes a holiday to its diversity: Multiculturalism Day on June 27.

Said former U.S. President Bill Clinton: *"In a world darkened by ethnic conflicts that literally tear nations apart, Canada has stood for all of us as a model of how people of different cultures can live and work together in peace, prosperity, and respect."*

That's largely true, but some Canadians feel strongly about what they perceive to be the treatment of people in their ethnic group. Ethnic relations have a long and complicated history in Canada, as students doing social studies reports discover quickly.

Modern life in Canada may have British and French fingerprints all over it, but neither country can claim

In May, Canadians celebrate Asian Heritage Month. There is an especially strong Asian community in Toronto—of the 2.6 million Asian Canadians across the country, half reside in Toronto. About 40 percent of Asian Canadians are Chinese, and almost a quarter are of East Indian origin.

People of Canada

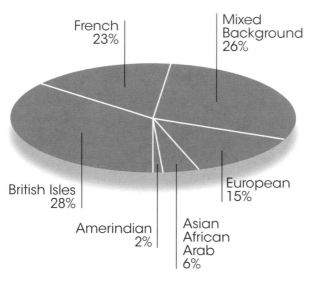

French
23%

Mixed
Background
26%

British Isles
28%

Amerindian
2%

Asian
African
Arab
6%

European
15%

Source: United States Central Intelligence Agency.
The World Factbook—Canada

although elected politicians run the country, Britain's Queen Elizabeth II is Canada's formal head of state, and the queen's image smiles from the backs of Canadian coins.

Canada's first settlers. As early as 20,000 years ago, humans crossed what was then a land bridge connecting Asia and North America. (Melting ice submerged the bridge eons ago.)

In time, European fishers began trolling Canada's opposite coast and ventured inland, meeting up with the Indians and trading fishing equipment for furs. Then, in 1534, explorer Jacques Cartier claimed Canada for France, but England wanted a piece of the country, too. The famous battle on the Plains of Abraham near Quebec City in 1759 placed Canada under British rule. Thus,

Questioning What is Fair

The British victory would seem to have settled things, but tug-of-war disputes continue today between segments of the population over issues of what land rightfully belongs to whom and how it should be governed.

French communities are sprinkled throughout Canada—primarily in Ontario, New Brunswick, and Manitoba—but it's French-Canadians in the province of Quebec who adhere most passionately to French culture and language. Quebec's city of Montreal is the second largest French-speaking

The Fête Nationale du Quebec, or Quebec National holiday, celebrates French-Canadian culture.

city in the world after Paris, France. Québécois, or Quebec's French-speaking citizens, keenly remember that the region was christened "New France" by French explorers. Some of these residents want to separate from Canada and establish the province as a separate nation operating outside of British rule. Although the movement is gaining traction, a majority of Quebec's citizens voted down attempts at separatism in 1980 and 1995.

The French aren't the only Canadians asking "What about us?" Canada's aboriginal, or native, peoples live in every province and territory, with concentrations in the prairie provinces of Alberta, Manitoba, and Saskatchewan, and on reserves. Their quest focuses on land rights as well as independent rule.

In 1982, the Canadian government officially recognized three aboriginal groups: the Inuit, who live in northern

How to POWWOW

Powwows are a way for aboriginal people to reflect on their past. Long ago, powwows were held so tribal bands could come together to meet and share traditions. After European groups gained control over the country, such gatherings were no longer permitted. Aboriginal people were forced to abandon their language and culture and made to adopt the European way of life.

Modern powwows were developed in the early 20th century as events for celebrations such as Canada Day. Today powwows allow native people to express their heritage and recognize their ancestry through song, drumming, dancing, storytelling, and art. Although most powwows take place during the late spring and summer months, they are also sometimes held in the colder months of October and November. There are powwows year-round in both Canada and the United States.

Powwows can be large or small, depending on the number of tribes participating. At the intertribal National Native American Veterans powwow in 1999, people from nearly 100 tribes from the United States and Canada came to honor Native American veterans. One participant said about the event:

"This is where you come and meet your friends. This is where you come to make friends with your enemies. This is a healing get together. This is where all nations get together and share their traditions and share words, wisdom, and stories. It's a learning experience."

Powwows and celebrations have traditionally been dedicated to warriors and a way of giving thanks for the gifts from Mother Earth.

In 1998, the Canadian government sent out a formal apology to aboriginal Canadians for the way they have been mistreated.

Canada, the Métis, descendants of First Nations tribes who married French and English traders and who now live in western Canada, and the First Nations, which includes all other native peoples that are not Inuit or Métis.

Today the native people living in Canada make up between 3 percent and 4 percent of the population and speak more than 50 languages. Nearly 70 percent of these belong to the First Nations tribes, 26 percent are Métis, and the remaining are Inuit. The establishment of Nunavut as a territory in 1999 was a victory for the Inuit, who make up 80 percent of the territory's population and run its government.

Rural residents likewise seek recognition. They express concern that government policies favor urban dwellers and overlook Canadians who live away from cities. Brokering deals that keep everyone happy is an ongoing task for Canada's federal government.

Canada's Cultural Mosaic

Sunday mornings are increasingly times when Canadian teens sleep in or at least do something other than attend a religious worship service. Church attendance is declining throughout Canada. According to a Canadian *Reader's Digest* poll, of the 71 percent of Canadian teens who believe in God, 18 percent attend a worship service once or more a week. Teens and their parents nonetheless maintain that faith plays a strong role in their lives.

Beliefs and means of worship vary throughout Canada. Many of the aboriginal peoples turn to native spirituality, as did their ancestors. And although a majority of Canadians identify with a Christian religion, there are also a number of other religious groups, including Sikh, Muslim, Jewish, and Hindu populations. Canada welcomes about 200,000 immigrants every year, and such diversity has been a characteristic of the country since its beginnings. In some countries, immigrants are made to feel that they need to change and assimilate to fit in with the rest of the country and become a part of the communal

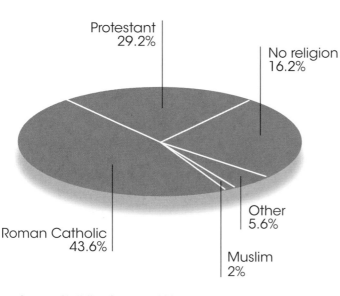

Religion in Canada

Protestant
29.2%

No religion
16.2%

Roman Catholic
43.6%

Muslim
2%

Other
5.6%

Source: Statistics Canada 2001 census

"melting pot." In Canada, however, immigrants become Canadians, but are encouraged to keep their own culture, adding to the country's multiethnic and multicultural "integration mosaic." In 1988, the country passed an act with the goal of preserving and enhancing multiculturalism by officially adopting the mosaic view of integration. Canada and Australia are the only two countries to follow such a policy.

After spending time with friends, family responsibilities, and religious services, there goes the weekend for the average Canadian teen. Alarm clocks get set again Sunday night.

Of the 23 million worldwide followers of the Sikh religion, about 250,000 live in Canada.

The Vancouver Polar Bear Swim takes place on January 1 every year. The first swim in 1920 had 10 participants. In 2007, there were 1,601 swimmers willing to brave the temperature. The coldest water recorded for the swim was 38 F (3 C) in 1928.

4

Pops to Poppies

THE KITCHEN TABLE IS STREWN WITH BRIGHTLY COLORED TISSUE PAPER, toilet-paper tubes, ribbon curls, glue, glitter pens, lipgloss, temporary tattoos, and strips of paper on which two sisters are scribbling amusing fortunes. They are making crackers for the youngest daughter's birthday. Crackers are classic party favors in Canada. Guests snap them open and little prizes tumble out. The family makes an extra fuss over the youngest daughter's January birthday, coming as it does on the heels of the Thanksgiving-to-Christmas stretch which, in Canada, spans three months.

Thanksgiving falls on the second Monday of October. With its northern climate, Canada's growing season is short, and its crops are ready to be harvested in early autumn. The Canadian Thanksgiving is an occasion for family and friends to gather in gratitude for the gifts of the land. Mostly, though, it's an excuse to overeat! The traditional feast piles plates with roast turkey, dressing, mashed potatoes and gravy, sweet potatoes or squash (sometimes drizzled with Canadian maple syrup), cranberries, and pumpkin pie.

Come October 31, the day revolves around candy. On Halloween, costumed youths go door-to-door trick-or-treating and scare-and-screaming. Kids consider Halloween a holiday worthy of a vacation, but school officials don't agree. Students have to wait until Remembrance Day on November 11 for the next no-school holiday. (Students in Ontario or Quebec have to wait even longer, since they don't automatically get Remembrance Day off.) On the 11th

Halloween is rapidly becoming one of the most popular holidays in Canada. More than $1.7 billion (U.S.$1.6 billion) is spent every year on treats, costumes, and decorations.

R.I.P.
ASHES TO ASHES
AND
DUST TO DUST
HERE LIES
SOMEONE
I WOULDN'T
TRUST!

R.I.
ASHES TO
AND
DUST TO DUST
HERE LIES
SOMEONE
I WOULDN'T
TRUST!

hour of the 11th day of the 11th month, Canadians pause to remember those who gave their lives during wartime. (World War I officially ended at 11 P.M. on November 11, 1918.) Teachers often have students memorize Canadian John McCrae's famous World War I poem "In Flanders Fields" or write to Canadian troops. More than half of all Canadians buy red poppies to wear on their collars and lapels by way of remembering.

Jingle All the Way

Canada is bound by its geography to celebrate Christmas, at least in the Santa sense. The country claims sovereignty over the North Pole, and Santa Claus is the guy at the pole. Christmas celebrations differ some from province to province, territory to territory, even door to door, as Canada's diverse populations put their own cultural spins on tradition.

French-Canadians decorate a tree on Christmas Eve and display a *crèche*, or Nativity scene, before attending La Messe de minuit, or Midnight Mass. In olden times, Roman Catholics fasted all day, which left them famished. So began the post-Mass tradition of *reveillon*, a huge banquet that might include the holiday meat pie known as tourtiére, meatballs, sugar pie, and *bûche de Noël,* a yule-log cake roll.

crèche
kresh

reveillon
rev-e-yawn

bûche de Noël
boosh day noh-ehl

In Flanders Fields

Canadian John McCrae (1872–1918) was a lieutenant colonel, a doctor, and a poet. Upset over the death of a friend and fellow soldier at the battle in Ypres, Belgium, McCrae scrawled 15 lines on a scrap of paper. It took him 20 minutes to write a poem that to this day stirs feelings about war and its consequences.

In Flanders Fields

In Flanders fields the poppies blow
Between the crosses, row on row
That mark our place; and in the sky
The larks, still bravely singing, fly
Scarce heard amid the guns below.

We are the Dead. Short days ago
We lived, felt dawn, saw sunset glow,
Loved and were loved, and now we lie
In Flanders fields.

Take up our quarrel with the foe:
To you from failing hands we throw
The torch; be yours to hold it high.
If ye break faith with us who die
We shall not sleep, though poppies grow
In Flanders fields.

To: Santa Claus The North Pole Canada, H0H 0H0

Every December, children throughout North America address letters to Santa Claus, in care of the North Pole. True to the mystery and magic of Santa, the North Pole sits neither inland nor on an island, but in the Arctic Ocean, which is almost permanently frozen. Canada claims the North Pole as its own, but there are 477 miles (770 km) of ocean between its northernmost point and the pole. Whichever direction you go from the pole is south. During the summer, the North Pole experiences 24 hours of daylight daily. During the winter, it's 24 hours of darkness. Lucky for Santa, he has travel plans every Christmas.

Visitors can reach the North Pole by airplane and ice-breaker boats.

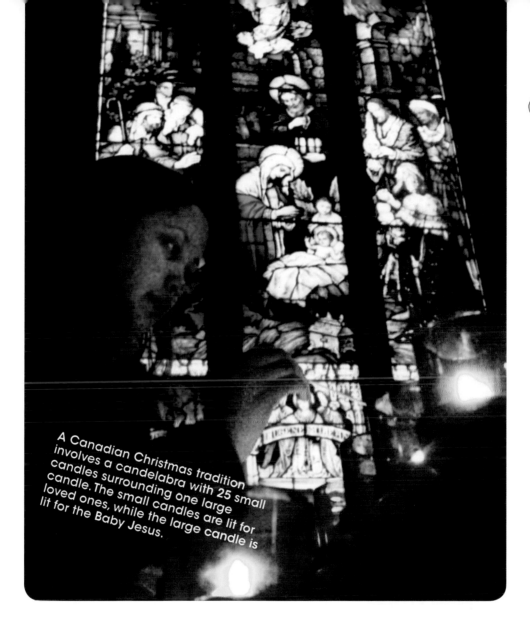

A Canadian Christmas tradition involves a candelabra with 25 small candles surrounding one large candle. The small candles are lit for loved ones, while the large candle is lit for the Baby Jesus.

Some teens may be allowed to stay up until dawn, but the fact they can doesn't mean they will actually have the ability.

For their part, British-Canadians hang pine boughs and kissing balls, and feast on stuffed roast goose or beef, veg-etables, mincemeat pie, and fruity pud-ding drizzled with brandy sauce. Turnips turn up in Labrador, not as a side dish, but as hollowed-out candleholders for the children. Fresh or smoked salmon may be served in British Columbia, and

Holidays in Canada

January 1: New Year's Day
February 14: Valentine's Day
Monday nearest May 24: Victoria Day
June 21: National Aboriginal Solidarity Day
June 24: Saint Jean Baptiste Day
June 27: Canadian Multiculturalism Day
July 1: Canada Day
2nd Monday of October: Thanksgiving
October 31: Halloween
November 11: Remembrance Day
December 25: Christmas
December 26: Boxing Day

turkey lands on many menus, including those of the Inuit, who also prepare caribou, seal, and raw fish. Inuit families gather in Santa's wake to throw harpoons, wrestle, build igloos, and race snowmobiles. Nova Scotia residents sing old British songs and carols to greet Christmas Day.

The Day After Christmas

Everyone is still humming Christmas songs on December 26—Boxing Day, so named because servants in the Middle Ages worked on Christmas but took the next day off. Then they received gift boxes from their employers. Boxing Day may also trace back to churches' custom of emptying their alms-giving boxes the day after Christmas and giving the contents to the poor. Today it's customary to leave gifts for newspaper and mail carriers, garbage haulers, doormen, tradespeople, and others in service jobs. Most stores are open, too, and after-Christmas markdowns cause a mad dash.

Beginning the New Year

At 12:01 A.M. on January 1, a commotion

of cheering, singing, and horn blowing can be heard throughout the country. The night before, people may have gathered together to celebrate the new year with singing, drinking, fireworks, and food. Many Canadians like to watch football or a broadcast of the celebration at New York City's Times Square. At the stoke of midnight, people may sing "Auld Lang Syne," a popular New Year's song in English-speaking countries, as a tribute to the past. Couples hug and

Shoppers wait three or more hours outside stores on Boxing Day, hoping to find bargains on after-Christmas specials.

kiss to begin the new year with love and friendship. Later in the day, the more adventurous join in the annual Polar Bear Swim. Participants dress in costumes to swim in British Columbia's English Bay. The water temperature at this time of year averages around 45 F (8 C). Anywhere from 1,000 to 2,000 swimmers show up, with another 5,000 to 10,000 spectators staying warm and dry on shore.

Weeks later, stores are a sea of red hearts for February 14, or Valentine's Day, another popular holiday on Canadian calendars.

Mindful of this, the sisters making party crackers set aside the extra red tissue paper and ribbons for Valentine's crafts later on. Today they have birthday on the brain. They put a cracker at each place setting and stick candles in the cake their mother baked. Homemade birthday cakes are the custom in many Canadian households. A wrapped coin is hidden between the cake's layers. The guest whose piece contains it goes first during party games. If the family lives in Nova Scotia, Prince Edward Island, or Newfoundland, the birthday girl has to worry about getting held down and her nose being greased. Scottish tradition maintains that bad luck can't stick to a slippery child.

Summer Warmup

More dignified protocol is upheld when celebrating Queen Elizabeth II's birthday on Victoria Day. Queen Victoria was

England's monarch when Canada was formed, thus becoming its first queen and holiday namesake. Her Royal Highness Queen Elizabeth II's natural birthday is April 21, but Canadians celebrate it on the Monday nearest May 24. Students get a long weekend

The first National Aboriginal Solidarity Day was held in 1996. Teepees are set up throughout the country to represent the aboriginal culture and attract the public's attention.

during which to cut loose at Victoria Day festivals, fairs, concerts, and fireworks.

Canada heats up in the summer—literally. Temperatures in the southern part average in the low 80s F (upper 20s C). National Aboriginal Solidarity Day is summer solstice on June 21, the longest day of the year. Drumming, powwows, traditional dances, native games, arts and crafts shows, and storytelling circles turn the spotlight on Canada's people of native origin and the rich contributions they to make to Canadian culture.

French culture takes the stage three

days later for Saint Jean Baptiste Day, or St. John the Baptist Day, secularly celebrated as Fête Nationale du Quebec, or Quebec Nationalist Day. Parade attendees and concertgoers wave Quebec's provincial flag and wear its blue and white colors. Revelers traditionally circle around bonfires until the wee hours of the morning. Only three days later comes Canadian Multiculturalism Day, on which Canadians embrace their country's diversity and commitment to democracy.

It all builds up to July 1—Canada Day, which celebrates the official establishment of the Dominion of Canada. Military pageantry draws hundreds of thousands to Parliament Hill in Ottawa for the changing of the guard, drills by the Royal Canadian Mounted Police

Canada's Historic Past

The name "Canada" comes from the Huron and Iroquois word *kanata*, which means village. On June 20, 1868, the provinces Nova Scotia, New Brunswick, and Canada were united as an independent dominion, or territory, of England. A holiday commemorating the union was established on July 1, 1879, as Dominion Day through a proclamation by the Governor General Lord Monck, asking for:

"*all Her Majesty's loving subjects throughout Canada to join in the celebration of the anniversary of the formation of the union of the British North American provinces in a federation under the name of Canada on July 1.*"

Canada Day has also been called the First of July and Confederation Day. In 1982, Dominion Day was changed to Canada Day by a Parliament vote. Some areas in Canada also celebrate Heritage Days to recognize the country's historical, cultural, and native heritage.

Committees are formed in each province and territory to plan and organize each year's Canada Day.

(the Mounties), Blue Angel aerial maneuvers, and, every so often, an appearance by Queen Elizabeth II. Throughout Canada it's a day for patriotism. Many families host barbecues, attend picnics, get their faces painted, and watch parades. When darkness falls, all heads turn skyward for fireworks. Sleep is the last thing on many Canadians' minds that night.

More than 46,200 tons (42,000 metric tons) of blueberries are harvested every year in Canada.

5

From the Land Comes Opportunity

CANADIAN TEENS AREN'T THE ONLY ONES SQUARING OFF WITH ALARM CLOCKS EARLIER IN THE MORNING THAN THEY MIGHT LIKE: Moms and dads also have obligations awaiting them. Fewer than one in five Canadian families can make ends meet on one income, so it's common for both parents to work. In fact, women comprise 57 percent of the Canadian workforce. Teens commonly fend for themselves at the breakfast table.

"Who drank all the milk?" is a morning outcry in many a household as teens pull almost empty milk bags from refrigerators. In Canada, milk is sold both in cartons by the liter and in clear plastic bags.

It can make for a mad dash in the morning as parents charge off to work. The unemployment rate is around its lowest in three decades, which takes some of the pressure off parents in terms of providing for their families.

Living Off the Land

Canada's landscape provides for its people on many fronts. Abundant natural resources generate jobs as well as energy, minerals, wood, and food. From Canada's rushing waters comes hydroelectricity. From deep within its core comes oil, petroleum, and natural gas, much of it as yet untapped. Forests cover 45 percent of Canada's land. From their sprawling acres come lumber, plywood, newsprint, and paper. From its

One of Canada's largest manufacturing industries is the pulp and paper business, both of which rely on a large supply of lumber.

Canada has 16 percent of the world's area of fresh water and four of the 14 largest lakes in the world, supplying a $5 billion (U.S.$4.7 billion) a year, 130,000 job industry.

mines, which number more than 200, come uranium and coal to fuel power plants, zinc and potash to make fertilizer, and a wealth of minerals—nickel, sulfur, titanium, gold, silver, platinum, lead, copper—to export, mostly to the United States. In fact, about 84 percent of Canada's total exports head to the United States.

Less than 3 percent of Canada's land is farming terrain, but 3 percent in a country as large as Canada is still three times the size of Great Britain. From this farmland comes an overflowing

Ready to Serve

For all its significance, farming provides jobs for only about 2 percent of Canadian workers. The big employer is Canada's service sector, which employs nearly 70 percent of Canadians in such areas as banking, insurance, finance,

Although wheat is the largest crop grown in Canada, tomatoes, canola, oats, and other foodstuffs are significant sources of production as well.

What's With the Wheat?

Support Canada! Eat lasagna! Canada supplies 20 percent of the world's durum wheat, and Italy is a big customer. Durum wheat gets milled into semolina flour, which is used to make pasta and couscous. The wheat grown for bread flour has a harder kernel and higher protein content. Become president of the Canadian Wheat Board and you're welcomed into the World Pasta Congress. Guess what's served at its events?

grocery cart. Potatoes, apples, and blueberries prosper in the Atlantic region. Peaches, pears, grapes, cherries, and plums flourish during the central region's mild summers, and maple sap drips bountifully during its springs. Barley, rye, flax, and wheat, lots of wheat, thrive in the fertile prairie soil. Beef cattle graze in the valleys and ranges of the Pacific region. And the fishing industry is strong on both coasts.

real estate, government, education, health care, and retail. Tourism leads that list, with one out of 10 Canadians working in a related occupation. About 80 percent of tourists flooding into Canada are Americans. Cameras click and dollars flow around Canada's cities, winter sports scene, and annual festivals. Canada's 42 national parks are huge draws and, as a result, hire scores of youth to work in visitor services, conservation, and back-office jobs.

Making a Name for Canada

Manufacturing and other industries keep close to 30 percent of Canadians punching time clocks. Ontario and Quebec produce more than three-fourths of Canada's manufactured goods, often shipping them via the Great Lakes— Superior, Huron, Erie, and Ontario— and the St. Lawrence River, which sees between $7 billion and $8 billion (U.S.$6.5 billion and $7.5 billion) dollars a year in U.S.-Canada trade. Canadian factories churn out machinery, computer gear, and telecommunications equipment, automotive parts, and motor vehicles. As teens itch for their own wheels being eligible in most provinces for driver's licenses around age 16— they might

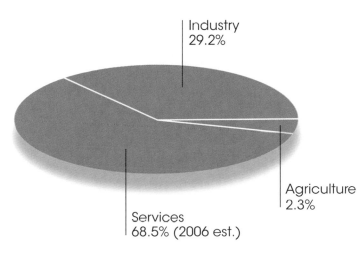

Division of Labor in Canada

Industry
29.2%

Agriculture
2.3%

Services
68.5% (2006 est.)

Source: United States Central Intelligence Agency
The World Factbook—Canada

Inventive Canada

Canada's minds are as productive as the hands that assemble its factory output. Because of the ingenuity of Canadian inventors, the world has telephones, insulin, and zippers. Other inventions include the pacemaker, the supportive Wonderbra, and the ever-delicious gravied fries-and-curds dish, poutine. Canada's infamous winters inspired the snowplow, snowmobile, and snow blower, with the ski binding no doubt a snowstorm brainstorm as well. The lives of businesspeople were made easier with the invention of the BlackBerry. Sports fans would be lost without the invention of basketball, lacrosse, the goalie mask, and the instant replay. And there's always been much to say into and about walkie-talkies. Over and out.

Snowplows are a well-needed invention. Canada receives between 10 feet and 40 feet (between 3 meters and 12.2 meters) of snow every winter.

About 110 million tons (100 million metric tons) of goods are shipped between the United States and Canada on the St. Lawrence River each year.

save to buy a made-in-Canada Toyota Corolla or a Honda Civic, Canada's most popular automobile. Van-driving parents might own a Honda Odyssey or Chrysler Grand Caravan, both products of Canada as well.

Attention, Young Applicants

Saving for a car, college, or anything else is made easier by the availability of summer or part-time jobs and made more difficult by the tempting presence of the world's largest shopping mall in

Extreme Shopping

Shopping is sport—extreme sport—in Edmonton, Alberta. The world's largest shopping mecca, the West Edmonton Mall, covers 48 city blocks and features 800 shops, 11 department stores, 100 restaurants, and 21 movie theaters. The thrills are dizzying: a 5-acre (2 hectare) water park with submarine rides, an indoor lake with bumper boats, a NHL-sized skating rink, a mini golf course, and an amusement park with 25 rides and other attractions.

The pirate ship is only one of the mall's features. There is also a water park with a beach, water slide, dolphin show, and even artificial waves.

Prince Edward Island has Canada's largest teen employment rate at 63 percent.

Edmonton, Alberta. Nearly one-third of West Edmonton Mall's employees are under 18.

"Student employment offers teens an opportunity to gain valuable employment skills, foster responsibility, meet interesting people, and helps build their confidence," says Anne Marie Robichaud, a staff writer for a parenting magazine. The most-coveted posts for teenagers are as ride operators and game attendants in the mall's amusement park, and lifeguards and slide patrollers in the water park. Alberta teens aren't, by provincial law, allowed to work between the hours of 9 P.M. and 6 A.M. They can, however, show up to work after school, weekends, and during the summer. Throughout Canada, almost half of Canadian teens ages 16 to 18 have paying jobs during the school year, with two thirds of them working for pay 10 or more hours a week during the summer. Teens can expect to earn in the neighborhood of $7 (U.S.$6.55) per hour: Canada's minimum wage ranges

Every summer, more than a million Canadian teens find ways to earn money.

from $6.70 (U.S.$6.25) per hour in New Brunswick to $8.50 (U.S.$8.00) per hour in Nunavut.

Teens ages 16 to 18 are actually the old-timers in the youth labor force. Children ages 12 to 14 who live in Alberta, for instance, can work up to two hours on schooldays outside normal school hours and up to eight hours other days, as long as they have a special permit. Each province sets its own age limits.

The food-service industry hires scores of employees between the ages of 15 and 24. In fact, youths make up nearly a quarter of its work force. McDonald's, one of Canada's largest such employers, offers discounts, paid vacations, and the chance to move up the food chain. Bill Johnson, who became president, chairman and CEO of McDonald's Canada, started as a crew person behind the counter more than 30 years ago. Employees at Canada's

FROM THE LAND COMES OPPORTUNITY

275-plus Rogers Video locations get free rentals, while employees of Shoppers Drug Marts' 900 Canadian stores receive staff discounts on merchandise.

Volunteering is also valued in Canadian culture, and about 60 percent of Canadian 16- to 18-year-olds choose to do so. Some even go abroad to teach, live, and study in a new country. Although not everyone has the same experience, one student's testimonial to his study-abroad time says it all:

"I couldn't speak the language. I was miserable for the first four months. Everything was bizarre. The food was terrible. I got sick ... it was WONDERFUL!"

Just Doing Your Job

The unemployment rate for the country is around 7 percent, and the rate for those with a university degree is 4 percent. Managers in just about every field—construction, transportation, health care, human resources, insurance, financial, real estate, manufacturing, information systems, sales and marketing, and correctional services—are in demand, too. As of 2007, job prospects in Canada are good, the highest category available, for the following positions listed.

- Aircraft mechanics and inspectors
- Ambulance attendants
- Civil, mechanical, electrical, and chemical engineers
- College and vocational instructors
- Computer engineers and systems analysts
- Contractors and supervisors
- Dentists and dental hygienists
- Firefighters
- Family and specialist physicians
- Judges, lawyers, and notaries
- Licensed practical nurses
- Medical technologists, including radiation
- Pharmacists, dietitians, and nutritionists
- Police officers
- Psychologists
- School principals

Canada is famous for its skiing and snowboarding resorts and trails. The 1988 Winter Olympics were held near Banff National Park in Alberta, and the 2010 Winter Olympics will be held in Whistler, British Columbia.

6

Homegrown Fun

GETTING EIGHT HOURS OF SLEEP A NIGHT ISN'T THE EASIEST THING FOR CANADIAN TEENS, given all the things that rev them up. Sports fever, for one, leaves players and fans replaying games in their minds as their heads hit the pillow. Screen time, too, eats into bedtime. Speaking of eating, Nanaimo bars—Canada's signature brownies that have a top layer of melted chocolate over a center layer of vanilla custard—produce a buzz and are best consumed when sleep isn't a priority. Saturday nights during the winter combine all three as Canadians gather in front of their TV sets, napkins in hand, to watch *Hockey Night in Canada*. The show airs double-header games and consistently ranks as one of the highest-rated programs on TV. Mark Cuban, the owner of the Dallas Mavericks basketball team, said, "More people watch *Hockey Night in Canada* on Saturday nights than watch NBA basketball on Thursday night in the [United] States. People in the U.S. don't realize that. They don't realize that there are more hockey fans in a country of (33 million) than there are NBA fans in the U.S. (population 300 million)."

Canada all but owns hockey. Canada is where hockey was invented in the late 1800s. The Stanley Cup, the top prize in professional hockey, came into being in 1893 when Canada's governor general, Lord Stanley of Preston, donated a trophy to a tournament in which his sons were playing. The official National Hockey League Hall of Fame is in Toronto, and the

Curling

Curling, a game played on ice with brooms and granite rocks, called stones, originated in the 1500s in Europe. More than 1 million Canadians participate in curling matches every winter—more than the rest of the world combined. The biggest competition of the year is the national men's championship, called the Brier. Over a quarter of a million curling fans flock to this event, and another 4 million stay at home to watch the event on TV. Famous curling enthusiasts include hockey player Wayne Gretzky and singer Shania Twain.

Curling receives, on average, 175 hours of television coverage a year—more than any other amateur sport in Canada.

NHL's all-time highest scorer, Wayne Gretzky, was a Brantford, Ontario, boy. Another ice sport, curling, is also extremely popular in Canada, drawing participants of all ages and scoring large television audiences. Hockey, however, elbowed it out as the "Official Winter Sport of Canada."

If there's an official winter sport, so must there be a summer one. In Canada, that would be lacrosse, which Indian nations and tribes played as a spiritual link to their Creator. Lacrosse is one of the few pieces of native culture to be passionately adopted by modern Canadian society. The first game between townsfolk and native people was in the 1840s. It was many years before the townsfolk won a game! Parliament named lacrosse as Canada's national game in 1859, and the Montreal Lacrosse club was formed in 1867. The club's aim was to standardize the rules and competition and to promote unity across the country. Its motto was "Our Country—Our Game."

Armed with long sticks, teens on peewee and bantam teams try to scoop up the ball, run with it toward the goal, and fling it into the net. Many teens watch the televised World Lacrosse Championship, which takes place every four years. The next championship will be in Manchester, England, in 2010.

Plugged In

When teens want to relax, they turn to the MuchMusic TV station, Canada's

71

Eva Avila was the Canadian Idol winner in 2006, the second female winner in four seasons.

Canadian Content

It's the job of the Canadian Radio-Television and Telecommunications Commission to monitor Canadian content, or "Can con." Its purpose is to ensure that Canadian programs are seen and heard by the public. Television and radio stations must present certain amounts of Can con each week.

Radio stations must ensure that at least 35 percent of their popular music selections are Canadian. French-language stations must guarantee that at least 65 percent of the popular vocal music selections they play each week are in French.

Television programs are defined as "Canadian content" if the producer is Canadian, if the key creative personnel are Canadian, or if 75 percent of the service costs and post-production lab costs are paid to Canadians. Private television stations and networks and ethnic stations must meet a yearly Canadian content level of 60 percent or more during the day.

spin on music television, or to reality shows such as *Canadian Idol*. The Canadian Broadcasting Corporation's programming includes the popular *This Hour Has 22 Minutes*, which is good for a laugh. Some shows produced in the United States are televised in Canada, but Canadian broadcasters are bound by strict rules to produce Canadian content, or "Can con."

Most Canadian youth prefer DVDs, the Internet, and electronic games over television. In 2004, 13 percent of

Internet users were between the ages of 12 and 17, and 97 percent of all elementary and secondary schools were connected to the Internet. Teens play and download music, e-mail, surf the Web, instant-message, and play games. When teens can't locate their friends online—horrors!—they give 'em a shout by speed-dialing or text-messaging their cell phones, which one in four students own. Parents comment that homework would take far less time if teens didn't conduct their social lives on the computer! About half of Weblogs, or blogs, are authored by teens between the ages of 13 and 19, and 10 percent of teens use the Internet to read other people's blogs. "Blogging is quickly becoming the 'teen' pastime of choice ... kids can connect and share their ideas with other young people," says Barbara McRae, a parenting coach. But the Internet isn't

In 2004, Canada ranked second (behind the United States) in Internet availability.

The Canadian Bookshelf

Bookshelves worldwide are richer for the works of Canadian authors, among them:

Margaret Atwood

The Handmaid's Tale and *Oryx and Crake*, novels of speculative fiction that question the use of biotechnology.

W.P. Kinsella

Shoeless Joe, a novel on which the movie *Field of Dreams* was based

John McCrae

In Flanders Fields, famous war remembrance poem

Lucy Maud Montgomery

Anne of Green Gables, set in the fictional town of Avonlea on Prince Edward Island

Farley Mowat

Never Cry Wolf, a novel made into a movie of the same name

Alice Munro

Her short stories often appear in *The New Yorker* and *The Atlantic*

Mordecai Richler

The Apprenticeship of Duddy Kravitz and the children's book *Jacob Two-Two Meets the Hooded Fang*, both of which were made into movies

just there for fun: Seventy-five percent of Canadian youth in grades 6 to 11 use the Internet for schoolwork.

Page Turners

The Internet doesn't rule entirely: Just check out the library books on teens' nightstands. Their stacks might contain *Al Capone Does My Shirts* by Gennifer Choldenko, *Kira-Kira* by Cynthia Kadohata, and *Red Kayak* by Priscilla Cummings. *Anne of Green Gables* might be in there, too. Author Lucy Maud Montgomery drew her inspiration for the story's fictional setting of Avonlea from the residents of Prince Edward Island. Like their peers worldwide, hordes of Canadian teens nearly stay up until dawn reading "One chapter, just one more chapter" of the

Harry Potter books.

Magazines and comic books are also popular bedtime reading. Teens hanging out at Canadian bookstores Chapters or SmithBooks pick up the latest issues of *Faze*, the largest teen

The Anne of Green Gables home on Prince Edward Island offers tours, a cafe, a gift shop, and a visitor's center.

Canada
Land use map

Land Use

- Cereal grains
- Dairy products
- Forests
- Livestock
- Manufacturing
- Non-agricultural land
- — Trans-Canada Highway

ARCTIC
OCEAN

GREENLAND
(Denmark)

Beaufort
Sea

Baffin
Bay

Labrador
Sea

Iqaluit

Whitehorse

Yellowknife

Hudson
Bay

St. John's

PACIFIC
OCEAN

Edmonton

Calgary

Vancouver

Winnipeg

Halifax

Quebec

UNITED STATES

Montreal

Ottawa

ATLANTIC
OCEAN

Toronto

UNITED STATES

0   200   400 mi.
0   200   400 km

N
W   E
S

magazine in Canada, or *Wet Ink*, which publishes original works by teens. Boys like *B-Zone* and *FUEL*. Comic-book hero *Captain Canuck* has been around since 1975. The most super of Canadian-born superheroes, however, is *Superman*. He is the co-creation of American Jerry Siegel and Canadian Joe Shuster, who based the city of Metropolis on his hometown of Toronto and *The Daily Planet* on the newspaper *The Toronto Star*.

Hit the Highway

There's a lot of Canada to see when teens shut down their computers and close their books and magazines. The Trans-Canada Highway rewards road-trippers with postcardlike scenery from one Canadian coast to the other. The world's longest paved highway, it stretches 4,849 miles (7,821 km) from St. John's, Newfoundland, to Victoria, British Columbia.

Driving it is a lesson in landforms.

The Trans Canada Highway connects Canada's 10 provinces.

Longest, Largest, Highest

The Trans-Canada Highway is far from Canada's only landmark that lays claim to being the "-est" in the world. Canada has the world's:

Longest Coastline

The Pacific, Atlantic, and Arctic oceans make up three of Canada's four borders and cover 152,100 miles (202,080 km).

Longest Shared Border

The United States and Canada share the longest common border in the world, with 3,138 miles (5061 km) on land and 2,376 miles (3,832 km) over water.

Largest Freshwater Lake by Area

Lake Superior, one of the Great Lakes, measures 350 miles (560 km) from east to west and 160 miles (256 km) north to south. It lies partly in Canada and partly in the United States.

Highest Tides

They roll ashore in the Bay of Fundy between Nova Scotia and New Brunswick at heights of up to 70 feet (16 meters).

Largest Skating Rink

Ottawa's Rideau Canal Skateway covers 4.8 miles (7.8 km), the equivalent of 100 end-to-end hockey rinks.

Tallest Freestanding Structure

High in the Toronto sky is the tapered tip of the Canadian National (CN) Tower. The world's tallest building reaches 1,825 feet (553 m).

The Trans-Canada starts in the Appalachian Region with its low, rounded mountains, and snakes by the lakes, streams, swamps, and forests of the Canadian Shield, Canada's largest land region. From there it goes (and goes) through the Interior Plains, or the vast prairies of middle Canada. Then it climbs over spectacular mountain ranges, including the Canadian Rockies, and traverses the Western Cordillera. From there, a ferry takes adventurers on their last leg to Vancouver Island and the Pacific Ocean.

Winter Playground

The Trans-Canada passes by Quebec City, but Canadians know to take a sharp turn into North America's only walled city. Quebec's winter carnival takes place during three weeks in late January and early February. The winter carnival—the world's third most celebrated public party behind Carnaval in Rio de Janeiro and Mardi Gras in New Orleans—colors the white landscape with banners, crowds, and street entertainers. Teens scramble to fit in all the carnival activities: the snow sculptures, ice palace, soapbox derby, ice tower, dogsled races, canoe races, night parades—everything! They jostle their way to Bonhomme, or "good guy," the carnival's enormous snowman mascot who talks, laughs, dances, and poses for photos for 17 days straight.

Locals sometimes skip carnival activities such as ice skating and skiing,

The annual Snow Bath (with the carnival mascot, Bonhomme, on the left) is a big part of the Quebec Carnival.

79

Canada
Topographical map

 Ski mountain

ARCTIC OCEAN

GREENLAND (Denmark)

Queen Elizabeth Islands

Ellesmere Island

Beaufort Sea

Banks Island

Baffin Bay

Victoria Island

Baffin Island

Labrador Sea

Iqaluit

Yukon River

Mackenzie Mountains

Great Bear Lake

Whitehorse

PACIFIC OCEAN

Yellowknife

Mackenzie River

Great Slave Lake

Hudson Bay

Queen Charlotte Islands

Lake Athabasca

Canadian Shield

Labrador

St. John's

Newfoundland

Vancouver Island

River

Peace

Marmot Basin

GREAT PLAINS

Churchill River

Cape Breton Island

Whistler/Blackcomb

Fraser River

ROCKY MOUNTAINS

Edmonton

Lake Louise

Banff

Apex

Lake Winnipeg

Laurentian Highlands

Quebec

Halifax

Vancouver

Calgary

Winnipeg

Great Lakes

Mont-Tremblant

Montreal

UNITED STATES

St. Lawrence River

ATLANTIC OCEAN

Ottawa

Toronto

UNITED STATES

0   200   400 mi.

0   200   400 km

N
W   E
S

Since its opening in 2001, more than 10,000 visitors have come to see the Hôtel de Glace in Quebec.

which they can do anytime. Canadians skate on frozen rivers and lakes. They skate on indoor and outdoor rinks. One million people each winter skate on the 4.8 mile long (7.8 km) Rideau Canal Skateway in Ottawa. They ski, too: Banff, Alberta, and Whistler, British Columbia, are famous downhill vacation destinations.

No matter where you're from, Hôtel de Glace west of Quebec City in Duchesnay, Quebec, is a novelty. The Ice Hotel takes 11,000 tons (9,900 metric tons) of snow and 350 tons (315 metric tons) of ice to build, an undertaking that occurs annually because, of course, the hotel melts every spring. The temperature inside its rooms, theme suites, cinema, and chapel is 25 F (minus 4 C), but warm whirlpool baths provide consolation. Overnight accommodations get reserved a year in advance. Day tours are an option for those who didn't plan that far ahead.

From daily media to weekly hockey to annual festivals, there's always something on Canadian teens' social calendars.

Looking Ahead

TEENS CALL IT A DAY AS NIGHT BLANKETS CANADA'S VAST AND VARIED LAND, darkening its eastern shore and spreading toward the opposite ocean. They set their alarm clocks and program cell-phone wakeups, mindful that tomorrow will inch them one day closer to their future as the country's visionaries, healers, and protectors.

There appear to be bright days ahead. Canada's robust economy, fueled as it is by abundant natural resources, will supply jobs and exports for decades to come.

With diverse populations spread out over great distances, unifying Canada won't be easy. Aboriginal groups seek self-government. Rural residents want to be heard. Moreover, rising costs pressure the health-care system. Canada's environment, too, requires tending.

As they ready for bed, teens might catch glimmers of green and red, white and blue, dancing across the night sky. The northern lights, or aurora borealis, are the heavens' gift to Canada. They're a magnificent reminder that faith in the country and its youth is well-placed.

At a Glance

Official name: Canada

Capital: Ottawa

People

Population: 33,098,932

Population by age group:
0-14 years: 17.6%
15-64 years: 69%
65 years and older: 13.3%

Life expectancy at birth: 80.2 years

Official languages:
English and French

Religions:
Roman Catholic: 43.6%
Protestant: 29.2%
Muslim: 2%
Other: 5.6%
None: 16.2%

Legal ages
Alcohol consumption: 18 (19 in some provinces)
Driver's license: 16 (varies by province)
Employment: 14 (varies by province)
Marriage: 18 (varies by province)
Military service: 17
Voting: 18

Government

Type of government: Constitutional monarchy that is also a parliamentary democracy and a federation

Chief of state: Queen Elizabeth II; represented by governor general

Head of government: Prime minister is appointed by governor general on behalf of the queen

Lawmaking body: Bicameral parliament made up of the Senate (105 senators) and the House of Commons (308 seats)

Administrative divisions: Ten provinces and three territories

Independence: July 1, 1867 (union of British North America colonies) December 11, 1931 (independence recognized)

National holiday: Canada Day, July 1

National flag: Flag has two vertical bands of red with white square between them; an 11 pointed red maple leaf is centered in the white square

Geography

Total area: 3,993,868 square miles (9,984,670 square kilometers)

Climate: Varies from temperate in south to subarctic and arctic in north

Highest point: Mount Logan, 19,665 feet (5,959 meters)

Lowest point: Atlantic Ocean, sea level

Major rivers: St. Lawrence, Columbia, Mackenzie, Yukon, Nelson, Churchill, Fraser

Major landforms: Appalachian Region, Arctic Archipelago, Canadian Shield, Cordilleran Region, Interior Plains, St. Lawrence Lowlands

Economy

Currency: Canadian dollar

Major natural resources: Iron ore, nickel, zinc, copper, gold, lead, molybdenum, potash, diamonds, silver, fish, timber, wildlife, coal, petroleum, natural gas, hydropower

Major agricultural products: Wheat, barley, oilseed, tobacco, fruits, vegetables, dairy products, forest products, fish

Major exports: Motor vehicles and parts, industrial machinery, aircraft, telecommunications equipment, chemicals, plastics, fertilizers, wood pulp, timber, crude petroleum, natural gas, electricity, aluminum

Major imports: Machinery and equipment, motor vehicles and parts, crude oil, chemicals, electricity, durable consumer goods

Historical Timeline

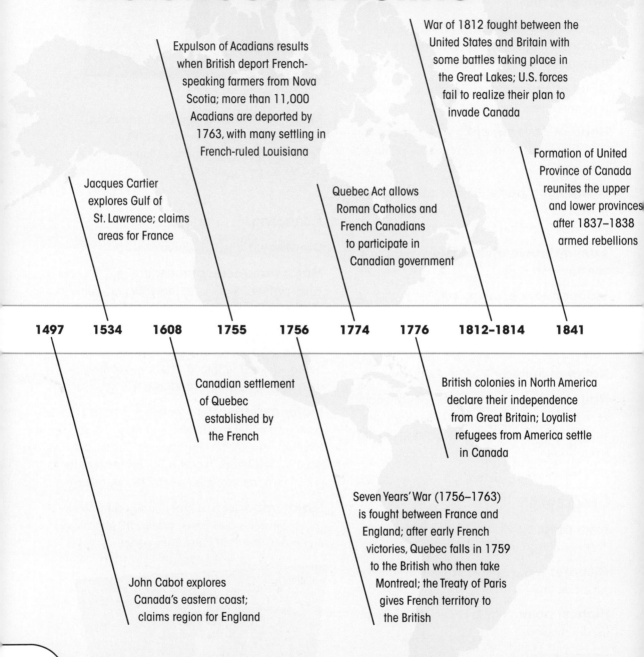

War of 1812 fought between the United States and Britain with some battles taking place in the Great Lakes; U.S. forces fail to realize their plan to invade Canada

Expulson of Acadians results when British deport French-speaking farmers from Nova Scotia; more than 11,000 Acadians are deported by 1763, with many settling in French-ruled Louisiana

Formation of United Province of Canada reunites the upper and lower provinces after 1837–1838 armed rebellions

Jacques Cartier explores Gulf of St. Lawrence; claims areas for France

Quebec Act allows Roman Catholics and French Canadians to participate in Canadian government

1497 **1534** **1608** **1755** **1756** **1774** **1776** **1812–1814** **1841**

Canadian settlement of Quebec established by the French

British colonies in North America declare their independence from Great Britain; Loyalist refugees from America settle in Canada

Seven Years' War (1756–1763) is fought between France and England; after early French victories, Quebec falls in 1759 to the British who then take Montreal; the Treaty of Paris gives French territory to the British

John Cabot explores Canada's eastern coast; claims region for England

Construction begins
on Canada's first
transcontinental railway;
the Canadian Pacific
Railway is completed
four years later

Slavery is abolished
in the United States; until
then, Canada had been a
major destination on the
Underground Railroad, a
secret network of people
helping enslaved people
escape to freedom

Canada acquires Manitoba
as fifth province followed
by British Columbia and
Prince Edward Island;
Northwest Territories
established

| 1857 | 1865 | 1867 | 1869 | 1870–1873 | 1875 | 1876 | 1881 |

Indian Act
declares who is
and is not an
"Indian," and
defines their
legal rights

Red River Rebellion between
settlers and Métis people (of
mixed European and Indian
ancestry); 1870 negotiations
lead to the creation of
Manitoba, rights for French-
language speakers, and
the promise of land to the
Métis people

Ottawa is chosen
as capital

First hockey game is
played in Montreal

British North America Act
unites Ontario, Quebec,
New Brunswick, and Nova
Scotia in the Dominion
of Canada

87

Historical Timeline

Yukon Territory established during the midst of the Klondike Gold Rush (1896–1899)

More than 1 million Canadians serve in the armed forces during World War II, and more than 40,000 die

Quebec's Quiet Revolution results in a more secular society, the creation of a welfare state, and the rise of nationalism among Francophones

Canada sends military troops to fight with the British and French in the Great War (World War I)

| 1885 | 1898 | 1905 | 1914–1918 | 1931 | 1939–1945 | 1949 | 1950–1953 | 1960–1966 |

Statute of Westminister gives British dominions, including Canada, complete autonomy

Canadian troops fight with United Nations forces in the Korean War

Alberta and Saskatchewan become Canada's eighth and ninth provinces

Métis people attempt to voice their concerns to the government about territory loss, and are nearly destroyed during the Northwest Rebellion

Canada is a founding member of NATO; Newfoundland becomes a Canadian province

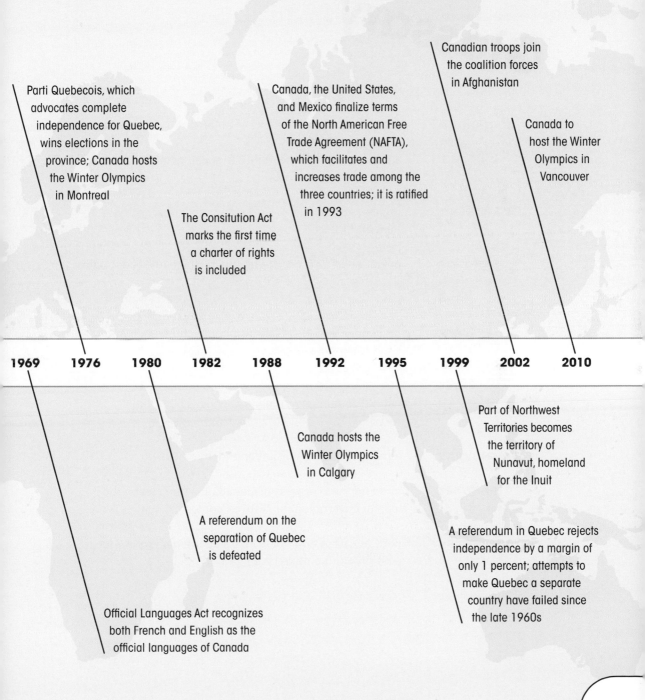

Parti Quebecois, which advocates complete independence for Quebec, wins elections in the province; Canada hosts the Winter Olympics in Montreal

The Consitution Act marks the first time a charter of rights is included

Canada, the United States, and Mexico finalize terms of the North American Free Trade Agreement (NAFTA), which facilitates and increases trade among the three countries; it is ratified in 1993

Canadian troops join the coalition forces in Afghanistan

Canada to host the Winter Olympics in Vancouver

1969   1976   1980   1982   1988   1992   1995   1999   2002   2010

Canada hosts the Winter Olympics in Calgary

Part of Northwest Territories becomes the territory of Nunavut, homeland for the Inuit

A referendum on the separation of Quebec is defeated

A referendum in Quebec rejects independence by a margin of only 1 percent; attempts to make Quebec a separate country have failed since the late 1960s

Official Languages Act recognizes both French and English as the official languages of Canada

Glossary

aboriginals	earliest known inhabitants of an area
bilingual	a person who has the ability to speak two languages with equal or near equal ability
First Nations	original inhabitants of Canada, with the exception of Inuit and Métis
immigration	migration to a country or region to which one is not native
Inuit	native people who live mainly in Canada's far north
Métis	descendants of First Nations people and French and English traders
provinces	10 regions within Canada that independently handle certain governmental services but follow national law
sovereignty	territories that exist as independent states
territories	three northern regions of Canada that are run by the federal government or Native Peoples
visible minority	not Caucasian and not from an aboriginal group, but possibly from a mixed background

Additional Resources

IN THE LIBRARY

Fiction and nonfiction titles to further enhance your introduction to teens in Canada, past and present.

Bruchac, Joseph. *The Winter People*. New York: Dial Books, 2002.

Montgomery, Lucy Maud. *Anne of Green Gables*. Wheaton, Ill.: Tyndale House Publishers, 1999.

Napoli, Donna Jo. *North*. New York: Greenwillow Books, 2004.

Paulson, Gary. *Hatchet*. New York: Aladdin Paperbacks, 1999.

Bowers, Vivien. *That's Very Canadian!* Toronto: Maple Tree Press, 2004.

Hughes, Susan. *Let's Call It Canada: Amazing Stories of Canadian Place Names*. Toronto: Maple Tree Press, 2003.

Pang, Guek-Cheng. *Canada*. New York: Benchmark Books, 2004.

ON THE WEB

For more information on this topic, use FactHound.

1. Go to www.facthound.com
2. Type in this book ID: 0756533031
3. Click on the *Fetch It* button.

Look for more Global Connections books.

Teens in Australia
Teens in Brazil
Teens in China
Teens in Egypt
Teens in England
Teens in France
Teens in India

Teens in Iran
Teens in Israel
Teens in Japan
Teens in Kenya
Teens in Mexico
Teens in Nigeria
Teens in Russia

Teens in Saudi Arabia
Teens in South Korea
Teens in Spain
Teens in Venezuela
Teens in Vietnam

Source Notes

Page 12, sidebar, line 8: Keith C. Heidorn. "Life at Minus 80: The Men of Snag." The Weather Doctor: Weather Events. 1 Feb. 2002. 15 April 2007. www.islandnet.com/~see/weather/events/life-80.htm

Page 26, column 2, line 15: "Unsocialized Medicine: A Landmark Ruling Exposes Canada's Health-Care Inequality." The Opinion Journal. 13 May 2005. 5 April 2007. www.opinionjournal.com/editorial/feature.html?id=110006813

Page 29, sidebar, line 12: Renee Alexander. "Tim Hortons: Power Play." BrandChannel.com. 10 Oct. 2005. 3 March 2007. www.brandchannel.com/features_profile.asp?pr_id=253

Page 36, sidebar, line 1: Alexander Panetta. "Canada Votes to Allow Gay Marriage." ILGA Files: Same-Sex Marriage. 29 June 2005. 3 March 2007. www.ilga.org/news_results.asp?LanguageID=1&FileCategory=3&FileID=658

Page 37, column 2, line 2: John Gray. "Was the American Ambassador Meddling in a Canadian Election?" Canada Votes 2006. 14 Dec. 2005. 18 March 2007. www.cbc.ca/canadavotes/realitycheck/americans.html

Page 40, sidebar, column 2: Rudi Williams. "A Powwow is Meeting, Making Friends and Spiritual Renewal." American Forces Press Service. 20 Nov. 1998. 4 March 2007. www.defenselink.mil/news/newsarticle.aspx?id=43266

Page 42, chart, line 1: "Census of Population: Income of individuals, families and households; religion." The Daily. Statistics Canada. 13 May 2003. 7 May 2007. www.statcan.ca/Daily/English/030513/d030513a.htm

Page 54, sidebar, column 1, line 12: "Dominion Day." Canadian Heritage. 4 March 2003. 10 April 2007. www.pch.gc.ca/progs/cpsc-ccsp/jfa-ha/dominion_e.cfm

Page 65, column 1, line 4: Anne Marie Robichaud. "Preparing Teenagers for Their First Summer Job." CanadianParents.com. 16 August 2004. www.canadianparents.com/CPO/TweensTeens/Teens/2004/08/16/592445.html

Page 67, column 2, line 5: Alan Cumyn. "So—You Want to go Abroad ... " Canadian Bureau for International Organization: Destination Education. www.destineducation.ca/cdnstdnt/witwigo_e.htm

Page 69, column 2, line 11: Dave Feschuk. "Cuban's Message to NHL: NHL Could Compete with NBA in U.S." The Toronto Star. 16 Jan. 2007. www.thestar.com/article/171418

Page 73, column 2, line 7: Barbara McRae. "The Truth About Teen Blogging." TeenFrontier.com. 10 January 2006. 5 April 2007. www.canadianparents.com/CPO/TweensTeens/Teens/2006/01/10/1387572.html

Pages 84-85, At a Glance: United States Central Intelligence Agency. The World Factbook—Canada. 17 April 2007. 25 April 2007. www.cia.gov/library/publications/the-world-factbook/geos/ca.html

Select Bibliography

Cameron, Elspeth. *Multiculturalism and Immigration in Canada: An Introductory Reader.* Toronto: Canadian Scholars Press, 2004.

Contemporary Authors Online. Gale, 2007. Reproduced in *Biography Resource Center*. Farmington Hills, Mich.: Thomson Gale, 2007.

Frommer's Canada. New York: Macmillan Travel, 1996.

Getis, Arthur. *The United States and Canada: The Land and the People*. Boston: McGraw-Hill, 2001.

Kreuzer, Terese Loeb. *How to Move to Canada: A Primer for Americans*. New York: Thomas Dunne Books, 2006.

"Margaret (Eleanor) Atwood." *Contemporary Novelists, 7th Ed*. St. James Press, 2001. Reproduced in *Biography Resource Center*. Farmington Hills, Mich.: Thomson Gale, 2007.

Reindeau, Roger E. *A Brief History of Canada*. New York: Facts on File, 2007.

Index

About the Author
Kitty Shea

Kitty Shea founded Ideas & Words in 1988 with the goal of following her curiosity into different writing disciplines and subject matter. She has since authored books for young readers, served as editor of home and travel magazines, edited cookbooks, and published hundreds of articles and essays. Kitty Shea has also taught in the journalism department of her alma mater, the University of St. Thomas in St. Paul, Minnesota.

About the Content Adviser
Miriam Kaufman

Our content adviser, Miriam Kaufman, M.D., is a pediatrician at Toronto's Hospital for Sick Children and an associate professor at the University of Toronto. She specializes in teens who have chronic illnesses and disabilities and has written books and articles for teens and their parents. Dr. Kaufman is also a frequent speaker at schools, conferences, and in the media.